The month of September, from the illuminated manuscript
Les Très Riches Heures du duc de Berry

The Story of a Special Day
Volume 256

September

12

255th day of the year
(256th in leap years)
110 days remaining
until the end of the year.

by Michael Dobson

Timespinner
Press

This book is also available in e-book form for Kindle, e-pub devices, and other formats from your favorite online booksellers.

For more information about the series, about us, or about your special day, please email us at editor@timespinnerpress.com.

Look for other volumes in *The Story of a Special Day*, coming often. See www.timespinnerpress.com for details and for the most recent information.

Table of Contents

Cover: Ancient black-figure Greek helm representing the Battle of Marathon — for the *Event of the Day.*

Back Cover and Frontispiece: The month of July, from the French Gothic illuminated manuscript *Les Très Riches Heures du duc de Berry.*

September 12
Quotations

"I believe that it is better to tell the truth than to lie. I believe that it is better to be free than to be a slave. And I believe that it is better to know than be ignorant."

— *H. L. Mencken, born September 12, 1880*

"The battles that count aren't the ones for gold medals. The struggles within yourself — the invisible, inevitable battles inside all of us — that's where it's at."

— *Jesse Owens, born September 12, 1913*

"He who has had, has been, but he who hasn't been, has been had."

— *Stanisław Lem, born September 12, 1921*

"It is better to die for an idea that will live, than to live for an idea that will die."

— *Steve Biko, killed September 12, 1977*

"You can ask the people around me. I don't give up. I don't give up...and it's not out of frustration and desperation that I say I don't give up. I don't give up because I don't give up. I don't believe in it."

— *Johnny Cash, died September 12, 2003*

Event of the Day
The Battle of Marathon

On September 12, 490 BCE, the fate of western civilization hung in the balance. A massive army under the command of Darius I, King of Persia, planned to subjugate Greece under Persian rule. Enraged because the Greeks had aided the cities of Ionia when they tried to overthrow Persian rule, Darius I had sworn to burn down the cities of Athens and Eretria.

The Athenians sent a force of 10,000 soldiers to oppose the mighty Persian army, consisting of up to 100,000 infantry, hundreds of ships, and 1,000 cavalry. Nevertheless, the Athenians succeeded in blocking the two exits from the plain of Marathon. For five days the armies were locked in stalemate, and then, under the veil of night, the Persians sent part of their fleet toward vulnerable Athens.

The Athenians were forced to attack, even though their forces were terribly outnumbered. But the Greeks had developed a new fighting formation, known as the *phalanx,* and their spear-wielding *hoplites* overran the lightly-armed Persian infantry.

When the battle was over, 200 Athenians and 6,400 Persians were dead, and the Persians retreated.

Although Darius I wanted to attack Greece again, revolutions within his own borders took precedence. It was not until the reign of his son Xerxes I that the

Persians were able to invade again — but with no more success than his father.

The Battle of Marathon was a turning point in the wars between Persians and Greeks, and foreshadowed the eventual Greek victory. That in turn led to the great Classical Greek civilization.

Not only is the Battle of Marathon a key moment in the history of western Europe, it gave its name to another enduring custom. According to legend, a Greek messenger named Pheidippides ran from Marathon to Athens with news of victory, after which he dropped dead from exhaustion.

Starting in the 1886 Olympic Games, the race from Marathon to Athens (about twenty miles) gave its name to the *marathon race*.

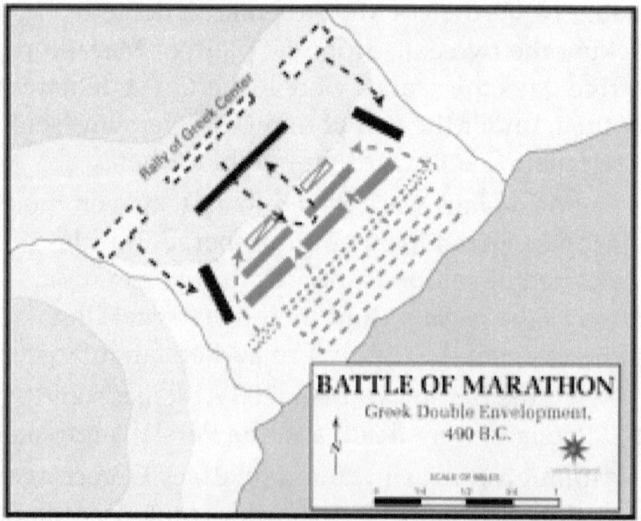

Map of the Battle of Marathon courtesy of the Department of History, United States Military Academy

September 12 Holidays and Celebrations

Defenders Day (Maryland)

A legal holiday in the State of Maryland, Defender's Day commemorates the defense of Baltimore on September 12, 1814, against an invading British force. It was during this battle that the events leading to "The Star-Spangled Banner" took place.

The Star-Spangled Banner from Ft. McHenry

National Day (Cape Verde)

Cape Verde, an island republic in the North Atlantic Ocean, celebrates its national day on September 12.

Day of Conception (Russia)

The Russian Day of Conception, also known as Procreation Day, urges Russians to produce children. Couples get time off from work, and if they have a child on June 12 (nine months later), they are rewarded by the regional government.

Programmer's Day (International)

Programmer's Day honors computer programmers. It is always held on the 256th day of the year (100 in hexidecimal, or 2^8), so it's held on September 13 in normal years and on September 12 in leap years.

Saint Patrick's Battalion Commemoration (Mexico)

In the Mexican-American War of 1846 to 1848, deserters from the US Army along with Roman Catholics from Europe formed the Saint Patrick's Battalion. Captured members of the battalion were sentenced by the US as traitors, and hanged *en masse* over several days in September 1847. Their sacrifice is commemorated in Mexico on September 12.

Christian Feast Days

In *Western Christianity*, saints commemorated on September 12 include Ailbe of Emly, Guy of Anderlecht, the Holy Name of Mary, Laisrén mac Nad Froích, and Sacerdos of Lyon. In *Eastern Orthodox Christianity*, it is the commemoration of Saints Cornatus, Sacerdos, Athanasius, Bassian of Tikhsnen, and Daniel of Thassius. (These are celebrated on September 25 by "Old Calendarists.)

What Happened on September 12?

1609 - **The *Half Moon* starts up the Hudson**

The *Half Moon*

Henry Hudson, an English explorer, was looking for a "northwest passage" between the Atlantic and Pacific Oceans, when he sailed his ship the *Half Moon* into the Upper New York Bay and then into what became known as the Hudson River, traveling as far up the river as the modern capital of Albany. Although he never discovered the Northwest Passage, he did establish Dutch claims to the region and helped start the fur trade.

1683 - **Battle of Vienna**

The Battle of Vienna, between the Holy Roman Empire and the Ottoman Empire, took place on 11-12 September, 1683, after Vienna had been besieged by the Ottomans for two months. The battle is famous for the largest cavalry charge in history. It also marked the beginning of the powerful Habsburg dynasty.

1846 - **Elizabeth Barrett elopes with Robert Browning**

After a secret courtship, made necessary by her domineering father, poet Elizabeth Barrett eloped with her lover Robert Browning, also a poet, and they were married in Italy on September 12, 1846. Both Barrett and Browning were already popular and well-known poets of the Victorian Era, and both went on to even greater fame and distinguished careers.

Elizabeth Barrett Browning (left) and Robert Browning (right), portraits by Thomas Buchanan Read

1857 - **The "Ship of Gold" Sinks.**

Carrying 550 passengers and crew as well as 30,000 pounds of gold from the California Gold Rush, the sidewheel steamer *SS Central America* was caught in a Category 2 hurricane off the Carolina coast.

Over the next two and a half days, the storm battered at the foundering ship. On the morning of September 12, 1857, observers spotted two ships nearby. About 150 passengers, mostly women and children, made their way to the rescuers on lifeboats. The ship sank later that day. The loss of the gold contributed to the Panic of 1857.

In 1987, explorers found the wreckage and salvaged over $100 million in gold. The book *Ship of Gold in the Deep Blue Sea* (1998) tells the story.

SS *Central America*, the "Ship of Gold"

1919 - **Adolf Hitler Joins the Nazi Party**

In 1919, following Germany's defeat in World War I, Adolf Hitler, a corporal in the German army, was ordered to spy on a small political party then known as the German Worker's Party. He quickly rose to become a leader, resigned from the army, and changed the name to the National Socialist German Worker's Party, or "Nazis" for short.

1933 - **Leó Szilárd Conceives the Idea of a Nuclear Chain Reaction**

Although the atom had been split by 1933, the idea of nuclear fission remained in the future. On Tuesday morning, September 12, 1933, physicist Leó Szilárd was waiting for a London traffic light. As he began to cross the street, he suddenly came up with the idea of a self-sustaining nuclear chain reaction using neutrons. While he later assigned his chain reaction patent to the British government, he also co-held (with Enrico Fermi) the patent on the nuclear reactor.

1940 - **Lascaux Cave Paintings Discovered**

On September 12, 1940, four teenage boys discovered the entrance toLascaux Cave. Going inside, they discovered that the walls were filled with paintings at least 17,300 years old, some of the best-known art from the Upper Paleolithic period. Opened to the public in 1948, it was closed in 1963 to prevent futher degradation of the art inside.

A cave painting of a horse from the Lascaux Caves

1942 - **Battle of Edson's Ridge Begins**

On September 12, 1942, the Japanese 35th Infantry Brigade attacked the US Marine forces guarding Henderson Field on Guadalcanal in the Solomon Islands. Over several nights, the Japanese attacked the defenders of the ridge again and again, and while they almost overran the Marine defenses, the attack ultimately failed, and the Marines continued to hold Guadalcanal.

US Marines returning from Edson's Ridge, 1942

1943 - **The Gran Sasso Raid Rescues Benito Mussolini**

A few weeks after the American invasion of Sicily, the Italian government deposed ruling dicator Benito Mussolini and secretly imprisoned him in a ski resort on high in the Apennine Mountains.

Under personal orders from Adolf Hitler, legendary Waffen-SS commando Otto Skorzeny located Mussolini. In a high-risk glider mission, German commandos landed in the mountains and overwhelmed Mussolini's guards without a single shot being fired, rescuing the dictator and achieving a major propaganda coup.

1952 - **Flatwoods Monster Incident**

The Flatwoods Monster, also known as the Phantom of Flatwoods, was first seen in the evening of September 12, 1952, when a mysterious light was seen near the town of Flatwoods, West Virginia. Witnesses saw a pulsating ball of fire, and next to it a strange creature, which immediately fled. The local sherriff reported it as a suspected flying saucer landing.

While various explanations, both normal and involving alien visits, have been proposed, the mystery of the Flatwoods Monster remains unsolved. Today, Flatwoods celebrates the "Green Monster" in a three-day weekend festival.

1953 - **The Kennedys Marry**

On September 12, 1953, future US President John F. Kennedy (then a congressman) married Jacqueline Lee Bouvier at St. Mary's Church, Newport, Rhode Island.

Jacqueline Lee Bouvier Kennedy at her 1953 wedding
(Photo: Toni Frissell)

1959 - **First Regularly Scheduled TV Show in Color**

On September 12, 1942, NBC premiered a new western, *Bonanza*, in "living color." The show lasted 14 seasons and was ranked as one of *TV Guide's* "50 Greatest TV Shows of All Time."

Cast of *Bonanza* (top to bottom): Lorne Greene, Dan Blocker, Michael Landon, Pernell Roberts

1959 - **Soviet Spacecraft** *Luna 2* **Reaches the Surface of the Moon**

On September 12, 1959, the Soviet Union lanched the *Luna 2* spacecraft (left), the first spacecraft to reach the surface of the Moon. It impacted the lunar surface east of the *Mare Imbrium* region.

1966 - **Gemini 11 Launched**

The ninth manned mission of Project Gemini achieved the first-ever space rendezvous with a target vehicle and achieved a world record high-apogee earth orbit. Today, the Gemini 11 capsule can be seen at the California Science Center in Los Angeles.

Gemini 11 Mission showing Agena target vehicle

1974 - **Haile Selassie Deposed**

After a reign of 58 years, Ethiopian emperor Haile Selassie was deposed in a military coup by the Soviet-backed Derg. Hailed as messiah by the Rastafari movement, the emperor spent his last years imprisoned in his own Grand Palace, and died the following year under questionable circumstances.

1984 - **Dwight Gooden Sets a Record**

In 1984, baseball pitcher Dwight ("Dr. K") Gooden of the New York Mets set a record with 276 strikeouts in a season by a rookie, shattering the previous record of 246 by Herb Score in 1954.

1994 - **Plane Crashes on the White House Lawn**

In the pre-dawn morning of September 12, 1994, pilot Frank Corder, suffering from depression, crashed his Cessna 150 airplane on the South Lawn of the White House, apparently in an attempt to hit the building. The only casualty, he died in the crash. The current president, Bill Clinton, was not in the building at the time because of renovation work taking place.

2005 - **Hong Kong Disneyland Opens**

Built on reclaimed land, the Hong Kong Disneyland opened on December 12, 2005. In 2010, it was the 15th most visited theme park in the world, with over 5 million visitors each year.

Who Was Born on September 12?

Actors and Actresses

Louis C. K. (September 12, 1967 —)

Stand-up comedian and television star Louis C. K., born Louis Skekely, starred in the FX comedy series *Louis,* which he also wrote, directed, and edited.

Amy Yasbeck (September 12, 1962 —)

Amy Yasbeck played Casey Davenport on the sitcom *Wings* from 1994 to 1997.

Rachel Ward (September 12, 1957 —)

British actress Rachel Ward won Golden Globe nominations for her roles in the film *Sharky's Machine* and the television miniseries *The Thorn Birds.*

Peter Scolari (September 12, 1955 —)

Actor Peter Scolari appeared in the television shows *Newhart* and *Bosom Buddies.*

Cynthia Myers (September 12, 1950 — November 4, 2011)

Playboy playmate Cynthia Myers appeared in Russ Meyer's *Beyond the Valley of the Dolls*, co-written by Roger Ebert.

Linda Gray (September 12, 1940 —)

Former model Linda Gray is best known for playing Sue Ellen Ewing on the television prime-time soap opera *Dallas* from 1978 to 1989, and has had numerous other television roles

Sir Ian Holm (September 12, 1931 —)

English actor Ian Holm was nominated for an Oscar for his role in *Chariots of Fire*, but may be best known for playing hobbit Bilbo Baggins in the *Lord of the Rings* film trilogy.

Sir Ian Holm

Desmond Llewelyn (September 12, 1914 — December 19, 1999)

Welsh actor Desmond Llewelyn (right) is best known for playing Q in seventeen James Bond films. During World War II, he was captured and held as a POW for five years.

Desmond Llewelyn

Maurice Chevalier (September 12, 1888 — January 1, 1972)

Actor and singer Maurice Chevalier is known for his signature songs, including "Thank Heaven for Little Girls" ad for his roles in such movies as *The Love Parade* (for which he received an Oscar nomination) and 1960's *Can-Can*.

Maurice Chevalier

Business and Manufacturing

Richard Gatling (September 12, 1818 — February 26, 1903)

American inventor Dr. Richard Gatling is best known for the Gatling gun, the first successful machine gun.

Gatling Gun

Crime and Punishment

Leonard Peltier (September 12, 1944 —)

Activist and member of the American Indian Movement, Leonard Peltier was sentenced to two life terms for first degree murder in the shooting of two FBI agents in 1975. His conviction is controversial in some circles, and was the subject of a 1992 Michael Apted documentary, *Incident at Oglala.*

Literature and Words

James Frey (September 12, 1969 —)

Author James Frey was involved in a scandal when investigators discovered that major elements of his autobiographical account of his struggle with addiction, *A Million Little Pieces*, were untrue.

Michael Ondaatje (September 12, 1943 —)

Sri Lankan-born Canadian novelist Michael Ondaatje won the Booker Prize for his novel *The English Patient*, which was made into an Oscar-winning film.

Stanisław Lem (September 12, 1921 — March 27, 2006)

Polish author Stanisław Lem was called "the most widely read science fiction writer in the world." His books have appeared in 41 languages. He is best known for his 1961 novel *Solaris*, which has been made into a movie three times.

Alfred A. Knopf, Sr. (September 12, 1892 — August 11, 1984)

Founder of the publishing house Alfred A. Knopf, Inc., he was noted for his attention to production quality in his books.

Arthur Hays Sulzberger (September 12, 1891 — December 11, 1968)

Sulzberger was the publisher of the New York *Times* from 1935 to 1961, a period of growth for the venerable newspaper. He succeeded his father-in-law, Adolph Ochs, in the position.

H. L. Mencken (September 12, 1880 — January 29, 1956)

Known as the "Sage of Baltimore," journalist and critic H. L. Mencken (right) is one of the most influential American writers of the first half of the 20th century. He was known for his sharp wit and controversial opinions.

Music

Jennifer Hudson (September 12, 1981 —)

Singer and actress Jennifer Hudson was a finalist on the television show *American Idol,* and went on to win an Oscar for her role in the 2006 film *Dreamgirls.*

Neal Peart (September 12, 1952 —)

Neal Peart is drummer and lyricist for the rock band Rush.

Barry White (September 12, 1944 — July 4, 2003)

Two-time Grammy winner Barry White was known for his distinctive bass voice and romantic image. His two biggest hits were, "You're the First, the Last, My Everything," and "Can't Get Enough of Your Love, Babe."

Barry White (Photo: King William)

Maria Muldaur (September 12, 1943 —)

Folk-blues singer Maria Muldaur recorded the 1974 hit song "Midnight at the Oasis."

George Jones (September 12, 1931 —)

George Jones has been referred to as the greatest living country music singer. He was married to country star Tammy Wynette from 1969 to 1975.

Politics and News

Scott Brown (September 12, 1959 —)

Republican Scott Brown was elected to the US Senate from Massachusetts in the 2010 special election to succeed the late Ted Kennedy.

Sam Brownback (September 12, 1956 —)

Republican Sam Brownback was a member of Congress, a US Senator, and the 40th governor of Kansas.

Stephen J. Solarz (September 12, 1940 — November 29, 2010)

Congressman Stephen Solarz served as a representative for New York's 13th District from 1975 to 1993.

Henry Waxman (September 12, 1939 —)

Representative Henry Waxman has been a US Congrssman for California's 30th district since 1975, and is considered to be one of the most influential liberal members of Congress.

Frank McGee (September 12, 1921 — April 17, 1974)

Television journalist Frank McGee was a leading NBC newsman. He hosted the second debate between John F. Kennedy and Richard Nixon, served as a rotating anchor for the NBC *Nightly News*, and as host of the *Today* show from 1971 to just before his death in 1974.

Science

Irène Joliot-Curie (September 12, 1897 — March 17, 1956)

Daughter of Nobel Prize winning scientists Marie and Pierre Curie and wife of physicist Frédéric Joliot-Curie, Irène Joliot-Curie (next page) won the Nobel Prize for Chemistry with her husband, for their discovery of artificial radioactivity.

Sports

Yao Ming (姚明) (September 12, 1980 —)

One of China's best-known athletes, Yao Ming played for the NBA Houston Rockets.

Irène Joliot-Curie (Photo: James Stokley)

Ángel Cabrera (September 12, 1969 —)

Argentine professional golfer Ángel Cabrera, known as "the Duck," is a former U.S. Open and Masters champion.

Vernon Maxwell (September 12, 1965 —)

NBA shooting guard Vernon Maxell, nicknamed "Mad Max," played for thirteen seasons. He is known for his clutch three-point shooting as well as for erratic public behavior.

Adrian Adonis (September 12, 1954 — July 4, 1988)

Keith Franke was an American professional wrestler known in the ring as "Adorable" Adrian Adonis.

Irina Rodnina (Ирина Роднина) (September 12, 1949 —)

Figure skater Irina Rodnina is the only pair skater to win ten successive World Championships and three successive Olympic gold medals.

Mickey Lolich (September 12, 1940 —)

Three-time all-star MLB player, best known for his pitching in the 1968 World Series, winning three victories for the Detroit Lions over the St. Louis Cardinals.

Glenn Davis (September 12, 1934 — January 28, 2009)

Hurdler and sprinter Glenn Davis won three Olympic gold medals and played football with the Detroit Lions.

Ernie Vandeweghe (September 12, 1925 —)

Retired New York Knicks player Ernie Vandeweghe chaired the President's Council on Physical Fitness and Sports and served on the Olympic Sports Commission. His son was an NBA All-Star. His wife was the 1952 Miss America.

Stan Lopata (September 12, 1925 —)

Major League baseball catcher and two-time All-Star, Stan Lopata played in 13 seasons for the Philadelphia Phillies and the Milwaukee Braves. He was the first National League catcher to wear glasses.

Tony Bettenhausen (September 12, 1916 — May 12, 1961)

Tony Bettenhausen won the automobile racing National Championship in 1951 and 1958, and started in the Indy 500 fourteen times. He was killed in a crash at Indianapolis in 1961.

Jesse Owens (September 12, 1913 — March 31, 1980)

African-American track and field athlete Jesse Owens won four gold medals at the 1936 Summer Olympics, held in Germany, enraging Adolf Hitler, who planned for the games to demonstrate "Aryan racial superiority." On his return to the United States, he was prohibited from commercializing his fame, and ended up in poverty. In later life he was rediscovered and was appointed a US Goodwill Ambassador.

Jesse Owens

Who Died on September 12?

Actors and Actresses

Tom Ewell (April 29, 1909 — September 12, 1994)

Actor Tom Ewell appeared in numerous movies and television series, but is best known for his role opposite Marilyn Monroe in *The Seven Year Itch*.

Raymond Burr (May 21, 1917 — September 12, 1993)

Actor Raymond Burr (right) is most famous for his roles in the television series *Perry Mason* and *Ironside*.

Anthony Perkins (April 4, 1932 — September 12, 1992)

Actor Anthony Perkins is best known for his role in Alfred Hitchcock's *Psycho* and sequels. He was nominated for an Oscar for *Friendly Persuasion.*

Literature and Words

David Foster Wallace (February 21, 1962 — September 12, 2008)

American author David Foster Wallace is best known for his 1996 novel *Infinite Jest,* named by *Time* magazine in 2005 as one of the 100 best English-language novels since 1923.

Robert Lowell (March 1, 1917 — September 12, 1977)

American poet laureate Robert Lowell won numerous awards and is considered a key literary figure of his generation.

Peter Mark Roget (January 18, 1779 — September 12, 1869)

British theologian and lexicographer Peter Mark Roget is best known for *Roget's Thesaurus,* originally published in 1852.

Military

Hugo Schmeisser (September 24, 1884 — September 12, 1953)

A German weapons designer before and during World War II, Schmeisser is famous for his improved machine pistol (Schmeisser-MP), the Stg44 assault rifle, and following his capture by the Soviets at the end of the war, his contrbutions to the AK-47.

Hajime Sugiyama (杉山 元) (January 1, 1880 — September 12, 1945)

Japanese Field Marshal Hajime Sugiyama was chief of the Army General Staff and minister of war for Japan during World War II. He committed suicide ten days after the surrender of Japan.

Gebhard Leberecht von Blücher (December 16, 1742 — September 12, 1819)

Prussian field marshal Gebhard von Blücher (right) led his army against Napoleon at the Battle of Waterloo. A popular German idiom, *"ran wie Blücher,"* ("charge like Blücher," or take direct, aggressive action), refers to him.

Robert Ross (1766? — September 12, 1814)

Major General Robert Ross led British forces in the War of 1812, most famously in the August 1814 burning of Washington, DC, which destroyed the White House and the US Capitol. Two American riflemen shot and killed Ross during the Battle of Baltimore the following month.

Music

Johnny Cash (February 26, 1932 — September 12, 2003)

One of the most influential American musicians of the 20th century, Johnny Cash (left), known as The Man in Black, was inducted in the Country Music Hall of Fame, the Rock and Roll Hall of Fame, and the Gospel Music Hall of Fame, for the range of his work.

Politics

Steve Biko (December 18, 1946 — September 12, 1977)

South African anti-apartheid activist Steve Biko is famous for his slogan "Black is beautiful." He died in police custody after being clubbed by his captors, and his death became an international *cause célèbre.*

Science and Technology

Jan van der Heyden (March 16, 1637 — September 12, 1712)

Dutch painter and inventor Jan van der Heyden helped revolutionize firefighting, inventing an improved fire hose, better fire engines, and a new organization for volunteer fire brigades.

Sports

Tommy Armour (September 24, 1894 — September 12, 1968)

Scottish golfer Tommy Armour, known as the Silver Scot, won numerous championships and co-authored the 1953 best-seller *How to Play Your Best Golf All the Time.* He was named to the World Golf Hall of Fame in 1976.

Spot Poles (December 9, 1887 — September 12, 1962)

Negro League outfielder Spot Poles was one of the fastest players of his day, with a lifetime batting average of over .400. He served in the US Army's 369th Infantry (Harlem Hellfighters), winning five battle stars and a Purple Heart.

The 1912 Negro League Lincoln Giants team. Spot Poles is in the top row at the far right.

The Month of September

The morrow was a bright September morn;
The earth was beautiful as if new-born;
There was that nameless splendor everywhere,
That wild exhilaration in the air,
Which makes the passers in the city street
Congratulate each other as they meet.

Henry Wadsworth Longfellow, "Tales of a Wayside Inn"

The Ninth Month

In Latin, *septem* means "seven," so it may seem strange that September is the ninth month of the year. The original Roman calendar, on which ours is based, started in March, making September indeed the seventh month. No one is completely sure when the start of the year was moved to January, but the traditional name of September stuck.

Romans also associated September with the god Vulcan, and thus expected the month to have fires, volcanic eruptions, and earthquakes.

In the northern hemisphere, September marks the beginning of meteorological autumn. In the southern hemisphere, September is the seasonal equivalent of March, the beginning of spring.

September and December always begin on the same day of the week. However, no other month in the same year will end on the same day of the week as September.

For countries that switched from the Julian to the Gregorian calendars in 1752, the date jumped from September 2 to September 14, meaning that there is no September 12 in that year.

September in Other Cultures

In Old English, the month of September was known as *Hāligmōnaþ*. Anglo-Saxons called it *Gerst monath* (Barley month) celebrating the barley harvest that would shortly be turned into beer.. In Finland, it is *syyskuu*, in Poland *wrzesień*, and in Greece Σεπτέμβριος. The Russians call the month сентябрь. While both the Hebrew and Arabic cultures have their own calendar system, the word for "September" is ספטמבר and in Arabic سبتمبر. The Azerbaijani call the month *Sentyabr*. In Hindi, the month of "sitambar" is written सितंबर. In both China and Japan, it's known as 九月, 구월 in Korea, and 腩朕 in Vietnam.

September Superstitions

"Marry in September's shrine, your living with be rich and fine."

September Symbols

Birthstone Sapphire, representing clear thinking.

Birth Flowers Forget-me-not, morning glory, and aster.

Forget-me-not *(moyosotis azorica)*

"Labors of the Month: September," by Simon Bening

September Events

August Moon Festival Celebrated by Chinese and Vietnamese people, the festival has been celebrated for at least 3,000 years. Its dates vary from September to October.

Eternal September In September 1993, when America Online (AOL) gave its members access to the Internet, existing users felt that the newbies ruined the experience. For these users, September 1993 has never ended, and is known as "Eternal September" or "September that never ended."

Football and School The American football season starts in the beginning of September, as well as the academic year in many northern hemisphere countries.

National Preparedness Month (US) Sponsored by the US Department of Homeland Security, National Preparedness Month is observed each September to encourage Americans to prepare for emergencies, including natural disasters as well as potential terrorist attacks.

Prostate Cancer Awareness Month A number of countries recognize September as Prostate Cancer Awareness Month. Its symbol is a light blue ribbon.

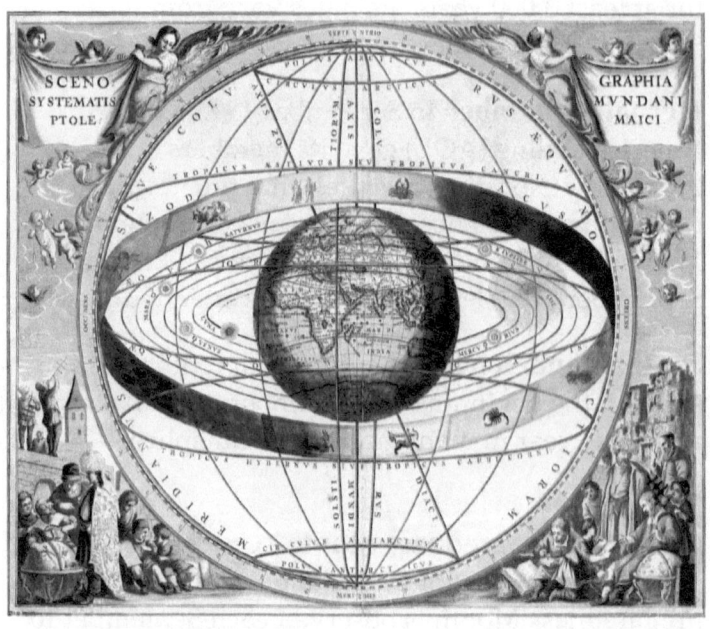

A map of the heavens showing the zodiac with the Earth as the center

September Zodiac Signs

From the perspective of someone on Earth, the Sun appears to move through the sky throughout the year, along a path astronomers call the ecliptic plane. The ecliptic plane is divided into twelve constellations, known as the zodiac, based on traditionally observed patterns of stars. On your birthday, you can't see your constellation, because it's in the daytime sky.

The zodiac was first developed by Babylonian astronomers about 2,500 years ago. Because they were unaware that the Earth wobbles like a spinning top (known as *precession*), they didn't make allowance for the fact that the Sun's path through the zodiac changes over time.

That means there are now two sets of dates for your birth sign. The *tropical dates* are the original Babylonian dates; the *sidereal dates* tell you where the Sun actually appears as it moves along its annual path.

For September 12, the *tropical* sign is Virgo, and the *sidereal* sign is Leo.

Leo

Tropical July 23 to August 23

Siderial August 16 to September 15

In Greek mythology, Leo, the lion, was killed by Hercules during one of his twelve labors. The easiest part of Leo to see in the night sky is an asterism known as the Sickle, looking a bit like a backward question mark. One of the nearest stars to Earth, Wolf 359 (just under eight light-years away), can be found in Leo.

In astrology, Leo is considered to be a fire sign. Traits associated with Leo are generosity, warmth, brightness, and self-motivation. Leos are supposed to be compatible with Aries and Sagittarius, and to a lesser extent with Gemini, Libra, and Aquarius.

Virgo

Tropical August 23 to September 22

Siderial September 16 to October 15

The constellation Virgo is the second-largest constellation in the night sky. Its brightest star, Spica, makes it easy to locate. If you can find the Big Dipper (Ursa Major), follow the curve in the Dipper's handle. The second bright star you see is Spica.

In Greek and Roman mythology, Virgo is associated with Demeter (Ceres), the goddess of wheat, and also with Erigone and Astraea. In astrology, Virgo is known as a "mutable sign." It's associated with being reflective and receptive to the ideas of others, sensitive to criticism, and oriented toward detail and precision.

Virgos are supposed to be compatible with Capricorn, Taurus, Cancer, and Scorpio, and to a lesser extent with Virgo and Pisces.

Illustration by Edward Penfield

What Day of the Week is September 12?

On what day of the week does September 12 fall?

Surprisingly, this isn't an easy question. Because the calendar year is 365 days long (366 in leap years), it doesn't divide evenly by the seven days of the week.

Also, the Earth goes around the Sun in about 365-1/4 days, so a calendar tends to drift over time. That's why the same date falls on different weekdays in different years.

This is made even more complicated by a change in calendars that took place in 1582. Our modern calendar has its roots in ancient Rome, in a calendar reform conducted by Julius Caesar. Caesar commissioned mathematicians to attack the problem, and they came up with the idea of *leap years*, and thus standardized the calendar for centuries to come. This was called the *Julian calendar.*

Over time, however, the small errors in Caesar's calculation compounded. That's why Pope Gregory XIII commissioned the *Gregorian calendar,* used in most of the world today. Some countries converted in 1582, when the calendar was first developed; some converted later; other still haven't changed.

Gregorian and Julian aren't the only types of calendars. The Hebrew year, the Islamic year, and many other calendars are used in different parts of the world and among different people.

You can convert Gregorian dates to other calendars, including the Hebrew calendar, the Islamic calendar, and even the Mayan calendar by visiting the Fourmilab Calendar Converter at http://www.fourmilab.ch/documents/calendar/.

Chinese calendar systems are quite complex and have changed several times; a full discussion is far beyond the scope of this book. If you're interested, you can find information here: http://www.hermetic.ch/cal_stud/chinese_cal.htm.

A 50-year brass perpetual calendar.

Copyright, Credit, and Contact

Follow Us

Our blog *Dobson's Improbable History* (http://improbhistory.blogspot.com) features short articles on events and people associated with each day, and updates several times each week. You can also get a daily "What Happened In History" message and all the latest Timespinner Press news by following us on Facebook at https://www.facebook.com/TimespinnerPress. Our Twitter feed @SidewiseThinker links you to all our News of the Day.

Contact Us

Find an error or a format problem? Want information about the series, about us, or about when the volume for your special day might be available? Please email us at editor@timespinnerpress.com. (We also take requests if your special day isn't yet complete. Please give us at least six weeks' notice if possible.)

On Dates

Historians use "CE" (Common Era) and
"BCE" (Before the Common Era) instead of the more
common "AD" (*Anno Domini*, or Year of Our Lord)
and "BC" (Before Christ), reflecting the fact that the
year-numbering system established by the Gregorian
calendar is used throughout the world in many
countries not culturally Christian.

The CE/BCE designation dates back to at least
1708, and has been adopted as a standard by the
United Nations and the Universal Postal Union.
Because this series of books covers events and
people of all nations and cultures, we use the CE/
BCE terms.

The abbreviation "O.S." ("Old Style") on some
dates refers to the fact that the Russian Empire did
not switch from the Julian to the Gregorian calendar
at the same time as the rest of Europe, and therefore
some figures and events have two dates. (See "What
Day of the Week..." for an explanation of Julian and
Gregorian dates.)

People and events whose original names are not
in the Western alphabet have their native names
(where possible) in the appropriate script shown in
parenthesis. If you are using an e-reader to access an
electronic version of this book, all characters don't
always display on all devices.

Sources

We owe a great debt to Wikipedia, which is our first stop for research. We attempt to make independent confirmation of all important dates and facts through a variety of other sources. Other sources we frequently use include the Library of Congress; "on this day" listings from *Encyclopedia Britannica*, the New York *Times*, and the BBC; and, of course, the always essential Google.

All art and photographs are either in the public domain, used under a Creative Commons license, or with a "fair use" justification, and most frequently come from Wikimedia Commons and the Library of Congress Prints and Photographs Division.

Attribution is provided where requested by the copyright owner or when of historical significance, listed below. For information about any particular illustration or photograph, please contact us.

Credits

- The illustration of the month of September used on the back cover and as the frontispiece is from the French Gothic illuminated manuscript *Les Très Riches Heures du duc de Berry* by the Limbourg Brothers, Jean Colombe, and an intermediate painter whose name is lost to history. It is in the public domain because its copyright has expired.

- Map of the Battle of Marathon courtesy of the Department of History, US Military Academy. It is in the public domain as a work created by the US federal government.

- The photograph of the Star-Spangled Banner that flew over Fort McHenry in 1814 was taken for the 1914 centennial, and is in the public domain because its copyright has expired.

- The engraving of Henry Hudson's *Half Moon* is in the public domain because its copyright has expired.

- The 1853 portraits of Elizabeth Barrett Browning and Robert Browning were painted by Thomas Buchanan Read. They are in the public domain because their copyrights have expired.

- Tllustration of the *SS Central America* is from *Frank Leslie's Illustrated Newspaper*, 1857. It is in the public domain because its copyright has expired.

- The photograph of a cave painting from Lascaux was released into the public domain by its creator, "HTO."

- The photograph of Marines returning from Edson's Ridge is in the public domain as a work of the US federal government.

- The photograph of Jacqueline Bouvier Kennedy at her 1953 wedding was taken by Toni Frissell. It is in the public domain because it was gifted to the Library of Congress by the photographer.

- The publicity photograph of the *Bonanza* cast is in the public domain because it was published in the United States between 1923 and 1977 without a copyright notice.

- The photograph of the Soviet moon probe Luna 2 is in the public domain as a work created by NASA.

- The photograph from the Gemini 11 mission is in the public domain as a work created by NASA.

- The 2008 photograph of Sir Ian Holm was taken by CossieMoJo at en.wikipedia. It is used here under the CC-BY-SA 3.0 license.

- The 1983 photograph of Desmond Llewelyn is by "Towpilot" and is used here under the CC-BY-SA 3.0 license.

- The 1920s autographed photograph of Maurice Chevalier is in the public domain because its copyright has expired. It has been modified for clarity.

- The 1876 photograph of a Gatling gun with the US 20th Infantry has been released to the public under CC0 1.0.

- The photograph of H. L. Mencken is in the public domain because its copyright has expired.

- The photograph of Barry White is by "King William" and used here under CC-BY-SA 3.0.

- The 1921 photograph of Irène Joliot-Curie was taken by James Stokley. It is in the public domain because its copyright has expired. The image has been cropped for this usage.

- The 1936 photograph of Jesse Owens at the Berlin Olympics is in the public domain because its copyright has expired and its author is anonymous.

- The 1957 publicity photograph of Raymond Burr from the CBS television series *Perry Mason* is in the public domain because it was published in the United States between 1923 and 1977 without a copyright notice. It has been cropped for this usage.

- The artist of the portrait of Gebhard von Blücher is unknown, but it was created circa 1815. It is in the public domain because its copyright has expired.

- The photograph of Johnny Cash was taken by Joel Baldwin. It is from the April 29, 1969 issue of *Look* Magazine. It is part of the Look Magazine photograph collection at the Library of Congress, and as part of the instrument of gift all rights were dedicated to the public.

- The 1912 photograph of the New York Lincoln Giants is in the public domain because its copyright has expired.

- The photograph of a star sapphire was released into the public domain by its author, Mitchell Gore.

- The chromolithograph of a forget-me-not is by Louis-Aristide-Léon Constans and originally appeared in the 1852-1853 edition of *Paxton's Flower Garden*. It is in the public domain because its copyright has expired.

- The illustration "Labors of the Months: September" by Simon Bening is from a Flemish Book of Hours published in the first half of the 16th century. It is in the public domain because its copyright has expired.

- The 1660 drawing of the heavens is by Johannes van Loon, and was first published in *Harmonia Macrocosmica* by Andreas Cellarius. It is in the public domain because its copyright has expired.

- The photograph of the 1906 automobile calendar by Edward Penfield is from the Library of Congress Prints and Photographs Division, and is in the public domain because it was published prior to January 1, 1923.

- The 50-year perpetual calendar photograph is in the public domain.

License Description and Terms

Aside from material purely in the public domain, photographs and other material in this book are used under specific licenses permitting free use, usually with attribution. For full text and terms of these licenses, click or enter the appropriate links below.

- Creative Commons Attribution 2.0 Generic (CC-BY 2.0): http://creativecommons.org/licenses/by/2.0/deed.en

- Creative Commons Attribution-Share Alike 3.0 Generic (CC-BY-SA 3.0): http://creativecommons.org/licenses/by-sa/3.0/

Timespinner
Press